A Gift
for You
from

_____

THE
APPLAUSE
OF HEAVEN

MAX LUCADO

THE APPLAUSE OF HEAVEN

Library of Congress Cataloging-in-Publication Data

Lucado, Max.
        The applause of heaven / Max Lucado.
            p.   cm.
        Abridged ed. in minibook format.
        ISBN 0-8499-5032-5
        1. Beatitudes—Devotional literature.   I. Title.
    BT382.L8 1993
    226.9'306—dc20   93-1914
                                                         CIP

3 4 5 6 9 PLP 9 8 7 6 5 4 3 2 1
Printed in Hong Kong

SACRED
DELIGHT

*C*ertain things about God are easy to imagine. I can imagine him creating the world and suspending the stars. I can envision him as almighty, all-powerful, and in control. I can fathom a God who knows me, who made me, and I can even fathom a God who hears me. But a God who is in love with me? A God who cheers for me?

*B*ut that is the message of the Bible. Our Father is relentlessly in pursuit of his children. He has called us home with his word, paved the path with his blood, and is longing for our arrival.

What is this cheerfulness that dares to wink at adversity? What is this bird that sings while it is still dark? What is the source of this peace that defies pain?

I call it sacred delight.

It is sacred because it is not of the earth. What is sacred is God's. And this joy is God's.

It is delight because delight can both satisfy and surprise.

*W*hat Jesus promised is not a gimmick to give you goose bumps nor a mental attitude that has to be pumped up at pep rallies. No, the Beatitudes describe God's radical reconstruction of the heart. The more radical the change, the greater the joy. And it's worth every effort, for this is the joy of God.

BLESSED ARE THE POOR IN SPIRIT

. . . FOR THEIRS IS THE KINGDOM OF HEAVEN.

CHAPTER TWO

*W*hat you want costs far more than what you can pay. You don't need a system, you need a Savior. You don't need a resume, you need a Redeemer.

Not through the right rituals. Not through the right doctrine. . . . Not through the right goose bumps. Jesus' point is crystal clear. It is impossible for human beings to save themselves.

God does not save us because of what we've done. Only a puny god could be bought with tithes. Only an egotistical god would be impressed with our pain. Only a temperamental god could be satisfied by sacrifices. Only a heartless god would sell salvation to the highest bidders.

*A*nd only a great God does for his children what they can't do for themselves.

That is the message of Paul: "For what the law was powerless to do . . . God did."

Those who taste God's presence have declared spiritual bankruptcy and are aware of their spiritual crisis. Their cupboards are bare. Their pockets are empty. Their options are gone. They have long since stopped demanding justice; they are pleading for mercy. They ask God to do for them what they can't do without him.

*A*dmission of failure is not usually admission into joy. Complete confession is not commonly followed by total pardon. But then again, God has never been governed by what is common.

$\mathscr{B}$LESSED ARE
THOSE WHO MOURN

... FOR THEY WILL
BE COMFORTED.

CHAPTER THREE

To mourn for your sins is a natural outflow of poverty of spirit. The second beatitude should follow the first. But that's not always the case. Many know they are wrong, yet pretend they are right. As a result, they never taste the exquisite sorrow of repentance.

$\mathcal{O}$f all the paths to joy, this one has to be the strangest. True blessedness, Jesus says, begins with deep sadness.

*A*s long as Jesus is one of many options, he is no option. As long as you can carry your burdens alone, you don't need a burden bearer. As long as your situation brings you no grief, you will receive no comfort. And as long as you can take him or leave him, you might as well leave him, because he won't be taken half-heartedly.

*B*ut when you mourn,
when you get to the point of
sorrow for your sins, when you
admit that you have no other
option but to cast all your cares
on him, and when there is truly
no other name that you can
call, then cast all your cares on
him, for he is waiting in the
midst of the storm.

*M*oments of comfort from a parent. As a father, I can tell you they are the sweetest moments in my day. They come naturally. They come willingly. They come joyfully. If I know that one of the privileges of fatherhood is to comfort a child, then why am I so reluctant to let my heavenly Father comfort me?

I am learning, though. Being a father is teaching me that when I am criticized, injured, or afraid, there is a Father who is ready to comfort me.

*T*here is a Father who will hold me until I'm better, help me until I can live with the hurt, and who won't go to sleep when I'm afraid of waking up and seeing the dark.

Blessed are the Meek

. . . for they will inherit the earth.

CHAPTER FOUR

*A*n ordinary night with ordinary sheep and ordinary shepherds. And were it not for a God who loves to hook an "extra" on the front of the ordinary, the night would have gone unnoticed. The sheep would have been forgotten, and the shepherds would have slept the night away.

*B*ut God dances amidst the common. And that night he did a waltz.

You can see the world standing tall, but to witness the Savior, you have to get on your knees.

*S*o . . . while the theologians were sleeping and the elite were dreaming and the successful were snoring, the meek were kneeling.

They were kneeling before the One only the meek will see. They were kneeling in front of Jesus.

Courage is an outgrowth
of who we are. Exterior
supports may temporarily
sustain, but only inward
character creates courage.
"They shall inherit the earth."
No longer shall the earth and its
fears dominate us, for we follow
the one who dominates the
earth.

*B*LESSED ARE
THOSE WHO HUNGER
AND THIRST FOR
RIGHTEOUSNESS

. . . FOR THEY WILL
BE FILLED.

CHAPTER FIVE

*A*dmission of thirst doesn't come easy for us. False fountains pacify our cravings with sugary swallows of pleasure. But there comes a time when pleasure doesn't satisfy. There comes a dark hour in every life when the world caves in and we are left trapped in the rubble of reality, parched and dying.

A ragged lot we are, bound together by broken dreams and collapsed promises. Fortunes that were never made. Families that were never built. Promises that were never kept. Wide-eyed children trapped in the basement of our own failures.

And we are very thirsty.

*N*ot thirsty for fame, possessions, passion, or romance. We've drunk from those pools. They are salt water in the desert. They don't quench — they kill.

$\mathcal{R}$ighteousness. That's
it. That's what we are thirsty
for. We're thirsty for a clean
conscience. We crave a clean
slate. We yearn for a fresh start.
We pray for a hand which will
enter the dark cavern of our
world and do for us the one
thing we can't do for ourselves
— make us right again.

*W*e usually get what we hunger and thirst for. The problem is, the treasures of earth don't satisfy. The promise is, the treasures of heaven do.

$\mathscr{B}$LESSED ARE
THE MERCIFUL

...FOR THEY WILL
BE SHOWN MERCY.

CHAPTER SIX

*R*esentment is when you let your hurt become hate.

Resentment is when you allow what is eating you to eat you up.

Resentment is when you poke, stoke, feed, and fan the fire, stirring the flames and reliving the pain.

Resentment is the deliberate decision to nurse the offense until it becomes a black, furry, growling grudge.

*F*or the one who tastes God's grace and then gives it to others, the reward is a blessed liberation. The prison door is thrown open, and the prisoner set free is yourself.

*F*orgiving others allows us to see how God has forgiven us. The dynamic of giving grace is the key to understanding grace, for it is when we forgive others that we begin to feel what God feels.

*T*he next time you see or think of the one who broke your heart, look twice. As you look at his face, look also for His face — the face of the One who forgave you. Look into the eyes of the King who wept when you pleaded for mercy. Look into the face of the Father who gave you grace when no one else gave you a chance.

*F*ind the face of the God who forgives in the face of your enemy. And then, because God has forgiven you more than you'll ever be called on to forgive in another, set your enemy — and yourself — free.

$\mathcal{B}$LESSED ARE
THE PURE IN HEART

. . . FOR THEY WILL
SEE GOD.

CHAPTER SEVEN

*F*irst, purify the heart, then you will see God. Clean the refinery, and the result will be a pure product.

We usually reverse the order. We try to change the inside by altering the outside.

When someone barks at you, do you bark back or bite your tongue? That depends on the state of your heart. When your schedule is too tight or your to-do list too long, do you lose your cool or keep it? That depends on the state of your heart. When you are offered a morsel of gossip marinated in slander, do you turn it down or pass it on? That depends on the state of your heart.

*D*o you see the bag lady on the street as a burden on society or as an opportunity for God? That, too, depends on the state of your heart.

The state of your heart dictates whether you harbor a grudge or give grace, seek self-pity or seek Christ, drink human misery or taste God's mercy.

*T*hose who have seen him can't seem to forget him. They find him, often in spite of the temple rather than because of it. They brush the dust away and stand ever impressed before his tomb — his empty tomb.

The temple builders and the Savior seekers. You can find them both in the same church, on the same pew — and at times, even in the same suit. One sees the structure and says, "What a great church." The other sees the Savior and says, "What a great Christ!"

Which do you see?

$\mathcal{B}$LESSED ARE
THE PEACEMAKERS

. . . FOR THEY
WILL BE CALLED
SONS OF GOD.

CHAPTER EIGHT

He built bridges by healing hurts. He prevented conflict by touching the interior. He cultivated harmony by sowing seeds of peace in fertile hearts.

*W*ant to see a miracle? Plant a word of love heart-deep in a person's life. Nurture it with a smile and a prayer, and watch what happens.

Sowing seeds of peace is like sowing beans. You don't know why it works; you just know it does. Seeds are planted, and topsoils of hurt are shoved away.

There is a canyon of difference between doing your best to glorify God and doing whatever it takes to glorify yourself. The quest for excellence is a mark of maturity. The quest for power is childish.

*T*he primary rule of thumb in the quest for power is never to stoop down for anything. Never stoop to appear weak. Never stoop to admit mistakes. Never stoop to help someone who could never help you. Never stoop to any level that might loosen your grip on your rung of the ladder.

The push for power has come to shove. And most of us are either pushing or being pushed.

*I*t might be the taking of someone's life, or it might be the taking of someone's turn. It might be manipulation with a pistol, or it might be manipulation with a pout. It might be the takeover of a nation by a politician, or the takeover of a church by a preacher.

But they are all spelled the same: P-O-W-E-R.

*W*hich would you prefer? To be king of the mountain for a day? Or to be a child of God for eternity?

*B*LESSED ARE
THOSE WHO ARE
PERSECUTED
BECAUSE OF
RIGHTEOUSNESS

. . . FOR THEIRS IS
THE KINGDOM OF
HEAVEN.

CHAPTER NINE

*A*nytime a person takes a step in the right direction, only to have her feet knocked out from under her, anytime a person does a good deed but suffers evil results, anytime a person takes a stand, only to end up flat on his face . . . the questions fall like rain.

*I*f God is so good, why do I hurt so bad?"

"If God is really there, why am I here?"

"What did I do to deserve this?"

"Did God slip up this time?"

"Why are the righteous persecuted?"

*C*louds of doubt are created when the warm, moist air of our expectations meets the cold air of God's silence.

*I*f you've heard the silence of God, if you've been left standing in the dungeon of doubt . . . . you may learn . . . that the problem is not as much in God's silence as it is in your ability to hear.

*T*his was Jesus' answer to John's agonized query from the dungeon of doubt:

"Go back and report to John what you hear and see: The blind receive sight, the lame walk, those who have leprosy are cured, the deaf hear, the dead are raised, and the good news is preached to the poor."

*B*ut note that Jesus didn't save John. The One who had walked on water could have easily walked on Herod's head, but he didn't. The One who cast out the demons had the power to nuke the king's castle, but he didn't.

*N*o flashing swords. Just a message—a kingdom message.

A unique kingdom. An invisible kingdom. . . . a kingdom of acceptance, eternal life, and forgiveness.

Does that mean that Jesus has no regard for injustice. No. He cares about persecutions.

*H*e cares about inequities and hunger and prejudice. And he knows what it is like to be punished for something he didn't do. He knows the meaning of the phrase, "It's just not right."

It wasn't right that the Son of God was forced to hear the silence of God. . . . but it happened.

*H*e sat in silence while the sins of the world were placed upon his Son. Was it fair? No. Was it love? Yes. In a world of injustice, God once and for all tipped the scales in the favor of hope. And he did it by sitting on his hands so that we could know the kingdom of God.

*R*EJOICE AND BE
GLAD, BECAUSE
GREAT IS YOUR
REWARD . . .

CHAPTER TEN

*H*ome. There's no door like the one to your own house. There's no better place to put your feet than under your own table. There's no coffee like coffee out of your own mug. There's no meal like the one at your own table. And there's no embrace like the one from your own family.

*F*aces of home. That is what makes the promise at the end of the Beatitudes so compelling: "Rejoice, and be glad, because great is your reward in heaven." What is your reward? Home.

When you look at this world, stained by innocent blood and smudged with selfishness, doesn't it make you want to go home? Me, too.

*J*ohn says that someday God will wipe away your tears. The same hands that stretched the heavens will touch your cheeks. The same hands that formed the mountains will caress your face. The same hands that curled in agony as the Roman spike cut through will someday cup your face and brush away your tears. Forever.

When you think of a world where there will be no reason to cry, ever, doesn't it make you want to go home?

In the next world, John says, "good-bye" will never be spoken. Tell me, doesn't that make you want to go home?

The most hopeful words
of that passage from Revelation
are those of God's resolve: "I
am making everything new."

*H*e restores my soul," wrote the shepherd. He doesn't reform; he restores. He doesn't camouflage the old; he restores the new. The Master Builder will pull out the original plan and restore it. He will restore the vigor. He will restore the energy. He will restore the hope. He will restore the soul.

When you see how this world grows stooped and weary and then read of a home where everything is made new, tell me, doesn't that make you want to go home?

reat," Jesus said, "is your reward in heaven." He must have smiled when he said that line. His eyes must have danced, and his hand must have pointed skyward. For he should know. It was his idea. It was his home.

You may not have noticed it, but you are closer to home than ever before. Every moment a step is taken. Each breath is a page turned. Each day is a mile marked, a mountain climbed. You are closer to home than you've ever been.

*B*efore you know it,
your appointed arrival time will
come; you'll descend the ramp
and enter the City. You'll see
faces that are waiting for you.
You'll hear your name spoken
by those who love you.

And maybe, just maybe — in the back, behind the crowds — the One who would rather die than live without you will remove his pierced hands from his heavenly robe and . . . applaud.